requiem

requiem

Joan Metelerkamp

DEEP SOUTH 2003

isbn: 0-9584542-1-3

deep south
p.o. box 6082
grahamstown
6140
www.deepsouth.co.za
contact@deepsouth.co.za

We gratefully acknowledge financial assistance in the publication of this book from the
Royal Netherlands Embassy

Ambassade van het Koninkrijk der Nederlanden
Neda

Some of the poems in this collection have been published in
www.donga.co.za

deep south titles are distributed by
The Univ. of Natal Press
www.unpress.co.za
books@nu.ac.za

Cover detail: The Strawberry Thief by William Morris

"A Requiem is a thing one writes for oneself"

(Schumann)

"The Power of Suicide

The potflower on the windowsill says to me
In words that are green-edged red leaves:
Flower   flower   flower   flower
Today for the sake of all the dead   Burst into flower."

(Muriel Rukeyser)

Eternal rest
requiem aeternam

Shoes with no feet
          shoes at the foot of the bed,
     legs, sleeves in the cupboard, shifting, waiting,
shoes: two puppies, or puppies' ears,
            listening, waiting,
        as the blood lies seeping,
sleeves: leaves crumbling
        against the stone
    of nose and jaw,
     shelf of ancient stone.

Hear my prayer
exaudi orationem meam

Listen   listen   listen
   three words I hear
     since you left

everywhere   whisper
   in all the silvery trees
     all trees   :   listen listen listen

see!   how the trees tear silver
   in the air
     the silver silver trees

Fires undying

ne perenni cremer igne

The night after they burnt your body
I burst through the door, dreaming,
I burst through the door, crying,

but they had brought her already –
"oh so you've brought her"
       I cried to the matron,
that sister, who handed me the baby:
"we were expecting you";

and I laid her in the basinette,
       laid her in the bath,
once for your mother, my grandmother,
once for you
(for a double baptism of fire)
for both times, twice, the water was fire –
fiery judgement, test of fire,
like living Raku firing
like the Christ-like corpse of a baby
corpse of Christ
like my children made at pottery one year
       for Christmas
       cradle of Christ

and the skin peeled away like coals
and the flesh of the new-born tender and clear

and the sister's, that matron's, instruction –
as when you learn to wash your new-born –

"call that woman, that artist,

that alchemical spirit
of artist
to see to the eyes:
for the one glows red,
the other white".

When you judge
dum veneris judicare

> "do you think you can shut grief in?
> what – from us? We who have perhaps
> nothing to lose"

(William Carlos Williams)

Not to mention it
  but in the poem
    that tells it as it is –

the prayer, not yet written,
  the one I cannot write
    the one that is taken away –

the one that draws us on with it
  lays it out,
    as in a cart

over rough roads
  as it should be
    before small town awkwardness.

*

sift through the old lines that have lasted –
  draw from the shelf of old books
    almost forty year old *Shopping with Mother* –

Ladybird book she bought, taught me to read
  what wasn't written: what wasn't spoken
    when to smile and keep silence: Mother,

not quite the bag and the hat
  but I stand on that threshold
    the place where you chose

almost the cardigan, almost the shirt,
  and what should I say in the hush
    of tissue paper folding?

*

take the words of our small town doctor:
  " … rough ride lately…
        mother passed away…"

oh Doc, you who know
  all the gradations of death,
    this was no passing, this was nothing away –

we do not know what to say –
  not the fact of the death, the gun in the hand
    held to the head,

but the freight
  of nothing to lose,
    every day.

Judgement day
dies calamitatis

Something, of how it is without you
I wanted to say –
(as you always knew it would be:

nothing,
finished, finished,
for we are the ordinary left living)

what to say – what is left
"I feel so…"
you said,

but before you had finished
I was up and away
thought I could get away

from that last sentence –

what is left – mist lifting,
trees standing,
cows in the field, cudding

legs cold with damp of grass, something,
something you wanted,
I want to say –

From the accursed

confutatis

They say
    that now you have gone
        the way your mother went

I must find my own – something – again –
    way – they say – something
        about a wound to the feminine,

toe the women's line
    as if they knew
        something about it,

some fairy-tale turn
    like line of doe's blood dripped, dropped
        in the bush;

myths, they speak in riddles like
    words lost in the forest,
        as if there were something

to find, as if there were some
    presence;
        they swing their sentences like

incense sweepers
    like celibate priests
        through the empty nave

but I – I am wild
    white belladonna lilies
        ripped limp from their rootings

Lamb of God
agnus dei

Love, there is nothing else for it, but
      love
         comes so clear

as I round the corner through the pass
      completely
        in the road

before me, like what we've always been
      looking for,
        the word,

like some vision, standing there, only
      there's nothing,
        of course,

only the hard presence of the word
      love, like the
        ordinary

surface, dirt road, pines on either side,
      there, close to
        Wessie's house,

sheep loose, rondlopers, on the hard road.

Who taketh away

qui tolis pecata mundi

And of course there is no forgiveness now
no-one to go to, to say
I forgive you do you forgive me?
and what to forgive?
nothing –
but all the living the living
keep from themselves keep from each other all the living
that drove you out
of your routine, up
from the table, into
your room, to the dark
cupboard with its stinkwood, secret
drawer...

always you told me
if we ever spoke of this at all
you had forgiven your mother
and I see now how it was: there was nothing,
no-one to forgive.

Have mercy

miserere nobis

I thought it would stop with me,
thought I could never do it,
even in my wildest dreams,

what your mother did to you,
Mother, what you did to me –
but she dreams I shut the door

on her: my daughter. Out there
with hyenas in the field –
"you had to do it for your

safety" she whispers to me,
as if her quiet reason
could cosset this cold stomach;

we thank God for her father,
who carries her for a while,
like a saint, on his shoulders,

but when he puts her down, dream
legs can't run, and at the hut
I have locked the door on her.

She tells all this: small voice of
morning's reason, cold quiet
of panic in retrospect;

we are driving through the dip,
rattling over corrugations,
"What? What?" I use the same voice

I used in my own dream, loud,
demanding, the night they burnt
your body, Mother: "What? What?"

I am shouting at you: for
Christ's sake speak up please, tell me
what in all hell has happened...

as you get up to give us
breakfast, close to the window,
so clear it is not a dream

but absolute, presence, you:
your green T-shirt, green collar
with the grey-green stripe, and green

of your garden behind you,
say: "I know you all loved me"
as if there could be nothing

more.

Deliver her from the depths
libera animas de profundo lacu

I stand in my new house, Mother,
first days of clear cold again
as if there could already be
      another winter, coming.

I stand in your green shoes
feet on thick soles,
wide enough
for your knitted socks,
     though this is already, another age

(come into my house, come in Mother,
knit socks if you like,
talk to me, tell me you are here,
help me with hems of cold curtains
where they drag across the bright floor)

see me, Mother, as I stand in your shoes,
black river below me,

river of dreams, river of blood, bedded in earth

see me, in your grandson's room
as I slide aside his curtains,
new, which we chose, still a child,
still wanting to show you
see the curtains with their delicate
fishes and suns, green moons
and blue striated like the sea?
wide curtains, drawn aside, to take in,
momentarily, taking your breath, drawing closer, clearer,

river's outlet to the sea.

*

running all night, all night without us, without telling us,
was it always, was it years, stiller and stiller,
into the bed, into the bed rock –

little words, little water-tight boat enough
funeral canoe, dug-out mokoro,
boat of words, take me to her:

steady paddles dipping,
procession of make-shift vessels,
paper boats, kissing the water,

river of black
stained with tannin of tree
iron of rock, salt of sea,
river of blood
waiting
for no-one, for nothing,
to the mouth
to the sea.

King of glory, we offer thee
rex gloriae, offerimus

Before it disappears
and while there is still time –
already it has almost burnt off
like the morning mist
(the bushveld before us then
and animals appearing
Nwanetsi so shy in the mist
we couldn't see the river we could hear)

already part of it, most of it –
burnt off –
strands hang around to remind me

while there is still time
and even if it is only a record –
emotion recollected in the spare
hour I have cleared, sparse clearing, clear
morning, frost burnt off, valley
below me, river clear,
familiar turns before me –

an offering –
a record –
I lay it out like sticks
like porcupine quills
shuffled and divided, striated sticks
thrown for the I Ching, calling for an offering,
clearing for the cautious king
to come in –

bare sticks:

record of a travel to the bushveld
record of return;
and words, words coming up for me, then,
too tired to hold them down,
letting them go, letting them, telling myself
there will be something new,
new words will take their place
new words like long grass
hiding humped buffalo
where, moments before, nothing
but the mist –

record of mourning –
always before us in the sand
flashing her emerald dots
that little dove, and then, now and then,
the one with the red eye and the black band
(but to have held the words, set them out, sticks burning
at the white heat
of mourning).

Lay it out, then, like burnt grass
of the highveld, standing like quills
at the edge of the vlakte, the edge of the high dry ground
grazed to stones,
ground we must cover
before the deep drop to the bushveld.

And there it is, the deep low,
there they are, the first evening, the three kings
swaggering along the road,
thin haunches, long strides, eyes bright before us.
And when is it, it dawns on me,

in this lush of concentration,
this thick of lowveld,
it is you, Mother, your story,
we are moving with;
long before
the homeward journey
the mile after mile wearing us to no resistance,
long before your grand-daughter flings her body along mine,
like logs, abandoned, limbs
abandoned
for her cry;
long before the words come
and go again,
like miles –

is it the old women of Timbavati, procession of
Appelblaar, Jakkalsbessie,
Kigelia, Acacia,
Huil – boer – boon,
tired arms, standing still,
in silence,
like the cold comfort of the Messiah's
chorus:
"and we shall change, and we shall change";

is it that the dry old river, Timbavati,
is running, full?
do you remember the time we walked
along its dry course,
and now it is full, Mother,
have you ever seen it like this?

But you cannot remember, we can tell you nothing,
we come offering what you cannot receive –
we can't tell you anything at all –
full arms, empty, tired at our sides –
not even how the old trees of Timbavati
stand there still

not how the flanks of quiet impala
quiver
in the sun,
not even the steely silver in your hand
how you held it,
for even that you do not know –
your own flesh –
Mother –
impala quiver
the river runs
trees stand despite tired limbs
the bush breathes,
bush breathes, smells,
bitter urine, dung,
old giraffes with abscesses
lick new leaves around the thorns –

the deep concentration of bushveld
as you dreamt of it
as you lay under your kaross
in cold post-war Cambridge:
to be in this bush and alive and dreaming,
woken by weeping
and again weeping for you
in the still warm of mid-day
among the starlings
and swept ground,

around the loose circle of camp rondavels;

your own last pilgrimage, last year:
cook, eat, sleep,
pick up and drive
across this slow sand
and through the dips –
grass, trees, butterflies, birds –
looking, looking like your grandson looks
deep in the bush
for hyena, he found for us, deep in,
while we waited, and coming out clear
jackal dragging through the long grass
heavy burden, body of bushbuck –
vultures' immense wings in silent sighs;

eight days with the dimensions of a dream
where nothing counts
but essentials
including consulting the books
and giving the names.

Come home to this:
aura of speechlessness like this split
brain of migraine that yesterday had me –
but again today it is almost clear –
black river below me running
to clear sea –
almost an opening
like the message of split sticks,
thrown sticks,
on the surface of the table,
calling
for an offering –

whatever I bring comes
too late
as and when it deems –
dimensions of a dream
remembered
in morning sun.

What weeping
lacrimosa

> *"I mourned, and yet shall mourn with
> ever-returning spring"*
>
> *(Whitman)*

A year already, and time
to move on –
for another speechless spring,
for even a year
and still what words are we left
for your parting?

In the dark, in the hour before morning,
I lie against your grand-daughter's warmth –
thirteen years, and she's let herself in
next to me;
I have forgotten the nightmare,
hold to the soft warmth,
the soft belly's ease;
five in the morning, and an hour at least
before the shallow cold comes
before consciousness starts me, leaves me,
like trying to hold it all in hand,
by myself.

But before,
before I catch myself thinking, remembering,
before that absolutely
soft-footed, for a shadow,
you are
somewhere, beside.

Down in your garden your husband now keeps,
fierce and determined,
all your softness is loose,
all your lace is all out,
all your first trace of celtis leaf
and arms-full of arums and all the annuals
you could never be bothered with.

Soon there'll be irises –
your favourites, your birthday flowers,
purple and faithful,
lined up against your bedroom window
unfurling their lilac like
all unknowing.

Day of wrath
dies irae

What I hardly wrote of was you,
real live you, while you were alive,
though always against or beside
or always you were the rip-tide
the reason, the argument –
what I rarely wrote of –
like wanting to write Rachmaninov's
second piano concerto, recovering every note
the wave of every note, and you were the piano player
your head hurting over the notes like shards
of flung crockery, black curls like bits
like argument, like torment –
god! Mother, though you never had black curls
never quite flung plates,
even at Christmas,
though your mind was sharper even than your tongue fuller even
than your hurt –
do you know how much it hurts last night I cried
in the dream again telling you absolutely straight
as a scrap of hurled plate: Don't do it.
Do you know how much it hurts.

Last day
dies illa

That day,
the last day,
up from the flu,
in your chair in the winter sun
you were working at William Morris's strawberry thief,

the last one, the last tapestry,
for your last dining-room seat –

outside the window, in that winter flowering tree,
your swee-waxbills on your seed-tray, sweet
carmine dash of crimson, buff, turquoise blue
as the gash of erithrina petal, cochineal against the clear,
against the sky,

stitches,
stitches;

we sat in the sun talking, your eldest son and I,
photographs, on the table,
art, worlds, words
between us, and you,
slightly to the side of us,
working with a silence
we couldn't hear

only one corner
one little bit of blue
left to do –

all that silence –

I'll tell you – I'll never do it for you:

all that I always had to undo

now that the words crumble
as specks, stitches of bread crumbs, as bird crumbs.

Deliver them from the mouth of the lion
libera eis de ore leonis

I dreamed the lioness you were –
for certain it was you as it was
                              part of me
as was the cub, the comforter,
                              part of me
lion cub like Little Bear
(like all those little elephants
falling in lines along the page like our little brother's tears,
as you read, all through the rest of us
   like Babar's, at the beginning,
                  when his mother was shot –)

cub's anthropomorphic arms around her –
                              ours and yours –
as the lioness wept, and the cub –

someone administered antibiotic:
the brave man, my husband, husbander,
and my son, whom I warned away –

lioness, wounded, mother, cub –

get up, grunting,
lick your shot –
make off,
into the deep.

interlude

Interlude

To Paolo

Perhaps this is a letter,
perhaps only the notes of a poem,
(not always the stand-in, poetry,

the afterthought, and the living voice
the connection – the living voice
and the presence of two people –

whenever two or three are gathered together
words to that effect,
the effect of presence)

you said: "I live in the present,
I have no thought for the future",
you said, "and less for the past" –

you said this on the same terrace
you had taken me to, seventeen
years before, like secrets, like essence

of longing, bruise of terracotta
dun against thyme, grey oregano
against crepuscular Tuscan blue:

before me like mother of mothers,
Florence, Firenze, sky deep so blue
behind and above San Lorenzo

sky so dark it was really night
Northern navy sky we don't get at home,
(sky of light, sky of cerise and wild white

we get at home, cerise immense
with screes of francolins and plovers,
lovers before nests, before dark)

you said: "I live in the present";
you in your shirt of Prussian night blue ·
and the bells behind you,

 as if our past had sloughed off all substance,
 this presence again serendipitous:
 here, sound, colour, hurt, love, scent.

*

Today I put on my red shirt,
terracotta cotton button-up shirt,
to take my father to Bologna –

wide-armed, open-armed in the square
"I could build like this!" he said.
"Only if you were of another century,

 and another country, and another age
– stage of your life – not to mention
another class" I finished it,

with that particularly correct
sententiousness of my post-
colonial countrymen.

Red city; city of riches
city of arches, of deep thrust
into the future, out of the blue;

grey, it was, and raining
and all the red of the city standing,
running, but like earth, like mud, like blood.

*

Sunday – San Gimignano –
(no fog, like the last time – no
cold of empty December grey and comfort

of stone – toc,toc of our feet on cold stone –
and the towers above us and grey
and our heat, our presence, between us)

Sunday was too-full tourists' town
and no-one, no body who belonged there.
But in the modern-art gallery

De Grada's objective reality:
sienna, sepia, greeny cobalt country,
trees, earth, stones, like hurt, like love;

"the best passport for the artist", Montale's
words: "look at De Grada, look at what he
looked at: this world, present, it exists".

*

In the dream I woke from, crying,
in the dream you came to me – angel arising –
(like the line of that poem) like the painting –

on Santa Croce's wall, Fra Angelico's :
the annunciation; but in my dream
your shadow on the wall and the shadow

of the woman between us
of the one whom you brought between us
to keep yourself from the need between us

shadow like an ideal, idea, from long ago,
like that shadowy cave wall – Plato's –
keeping us from the real, between us –

I called from the passage, forced-cheery,
"ciao ragazzi" – though there was something I needed
to tell you, something I had tried

to tell you, in fact, in reality
on the terrace, at supper,
to do with death, to do with my mother,

her suicide, the death of Eros,
the death of Jesus
that hangs all over this city –

hurt, I call it, love, but you said,
in the dream, it was all a whore-house
of a fuck-up, "un casino" –

like I walked into our faithlessness
seventeen years before like some body
that doesn't know its place doesn't know

where on earth she belongs, not enough
of herself to show you, not enough
then and like that now, too much left at home.

*

At home, where the dust blows like wild
cerise of ericas outside our windows,
husband and children wait for me.

*

In the Pitti – Nomellini's confetti
of light, mother holding her baby
up to the light, to the falling

of complimentary petals
(passion of red flecked through the white
and deep green) – "compleanno" –

complex of colour
like the cyclamen I carry to your dinner –
two decades' jade under your jacket collar

but the cord worn gold – vast night of gold
in the De Pissis collection – Ferrara –
golden night, artist and wife, larger

than life, husband and wife on their terrace –
flight of white splashed up the red of her dress –
foot prints, birds' body prints, absence.

What affliction
quid sum miser dicturus

What could burst a temple
        as if a gun were held to it
from within –

not the burning sun
on my arm
the sea haze
over the mouth
not the bricks against my back,
wooden humps, ridges beneath the thighs,
not these, nor the haze of the sea sky,
crickets, crows, cockerels' crows from below,
nor the valley, nor the river to the sea,
nor the warm air
I take in

tell me –

what can I tell you, Mother,
what could you have told me –

I know the tools – I've used them
as I've had them used on me:
quick
wit, the caustic sword – snicker-snack –
the wound licking door slamming sheathing.

What can I tell my daughter, Mother
(what you were taught
taught me)

what do I tell myself:
listen, ask,
let her be –

mornings like this you would phone me –

mornings like this and all the constriction –
what did I say – what was there for me to say –
(confusion I could call it, or ruthlessly, betrayal)
cold clichés
like "it isn't a daughter's task…"
to make out any more, what was muddier than water
thicker than blood…
told myself my own
something, something was more important –
what was it, Mother,
I can hardly remember.

Like this: remember
an afternoon, long ago, on the farm,
and the phone, the party line,
the hand cranked ring –
afternoon and the deep shade of the summer oak
and stillness within –
the phone ring, and you, talking –
how do I imagine the voice at the other end?
Beulah, mad woman's name,
mad woman in the musty decrepitude, crooked house, falling
shade,
                    constriction, crying –
what could you say –
how could you take your alcoholic neighbour
ten miles away on the dirt

in the middle of the afternoon
Tassies, Klipdrif, Angelica,
whatever you had?

Now the record
liber scriptus

(suicide notes)

Port Said, Mombassa –
names I heard as a child – whispers
sibilant as the sea's phosphorescence
as you swam through that luke-warm murk –
Mombassa, Tsavo –
three days from the ship
on the ten pound postal order
from your father;
Mocambique, Lorenco Marques, long before Maputo

when you were twenty and returning,
or twenty-one, and your mother –
no longer in trousers and scarf,
but lipstick, and new dress,
fit face for her husband's mistress –

nineteen fifty and fifty one
and the flowers so heaped on her grave
(clear shot
serrated square
as if I had never seen it there –
heaps, heaps of lillies,
the heaped body of the grave)

and you so young, Mother, so almost young,
coming back from Cambridge, from young men
(survivors, come back from the war,
war, you hadn't been allowed to give your
old newspapers, and your mother's knitting, or

your dreaded vests, for,
till Russia entered, your parents' loyalty spoken for);
photos of you on your way home
in Paris, and Florence,
all wide laugh and little frame
and everything before you
to come home to
Afrikaner nationalism, your parents' listing –
no voices in the dark drifting
no lying awake and listening
to the grown-ups wrangling
the raised tones of Iz, or was it Ike, the Trotskyite –

come home to
one brother's drinking
the other's dogged learning
all that present continuous competing, losing
to your mother's
dead end.

Come home to give up Law
to marry your farmer
give up your father's law
but not quite the latinate stoic he made of you:
Horatio holding the bridge
           while some of you, part of you
                              went under –

and then we are here
and our own remembering, beginning
within the shadow of your mother
utter, unmentionable, forever –

the stories you told us, and the notes you made
I found on your clip-board
amongst the photographs –
                    these things I know
not even knowing what I don't know
what it is I want to know
everything you didn't know how to look at how to see
how to come to, say:
                    this is yours,
yours, like your mother's, who couldn't come to it,
who took that little revolver,
the one that came round again to you,
you leave only the sketchiest of notes –
we knew all along.

Remember
recordare

Hot months, dry
and you not here –

holiday makers returning
my house filling
        stove burning

west wall leached of its sealing,
man lugging scaffolding –

months like constriction, like watching
your grand-daughter sit still to breathe
when she was little, and you, ministering –

in the dark, lights on the dust, up the hill, home-coming –
fiery throated night-jar in the warm road in front of us –

coming home, children almost asleep, breathing,
as we were, as children, on occasion
in the back of the station wagon –

in the back of the station wagon
as the sacks of young calves
on Monday mornings, weekly propitiation,
weekly boarding school –

and all our lives, somewhere, in the back of
all knowing,
somehow you would do it;
all Sundays all safety all everything
always coming to a close:

Sunday nights,
Sabbath blues.

I lie on my bed, breathless, head splitting,
husband and children down at your house –
Sunday lunch, "Granny's farm";

(last night the warm dark the lights soothing
the summer dirt road)

and always
you shoot yourself

Sunday lunch, Christmas, feasts, friends,
your flowered plates, your fast talk, loud laugh –
every morning you stood up again stood in the doorway
to your mother's suicide
all the days since the days
of the calves in the sacks, the young bulls, the abattoir,
the farm, the stories –

your grandmother's farm – Xanadu –
her Sunday lunch,
two austrolorpes, a sirloin of beef, five veg, puddings,
and uncles and cousins and stories –
you on your back on the back of the donkey cart,
    on sacks of lucerne

behind the Magaliesberg
the sun going down.

Deliver me
libera me

What happened to my body, Mother –
what happened to yours, what you did to yours,
I think this has happened to mine,
is happening to mine –

not age oh god that has so little to do with it
mother, more like it:
what happened to the body
that taught me to love, love
my body that I shared with love
what happened to that, Mother:

you lay on your bed on your back like cold shelf
cold thin yellow of all
you had run away from
you lay on your bed solid cold
of love having all run out
in cold blood
nothing whatsoever of you left
your utter body   abandoned.
Shoes at the foot of your bed still
not touching not even
rock lives so little.
absolutely you had abandoned.
what happened to your body.

Age has nothing whatsoever to do with it
only love. Love
give me back my body
let me take some body   to mine
god!

behind my bones, below my ribs
as if there were only one thing for it
and that is all.

When he sits in his chair, my husband,
saying if he's not careful he'll be finished by fifty,
meaning he feels finished now,
legs should get up and make their way there, lame body
slumped in its own chair
should break
open, over the arm
of that chair, should rise
again and again, take me
where the thick of life kicks in –

lie, then, on the path on my back in the sun,
like after love all abandoned
sun on the skin unprotected
like before the hole in the Ozone, like before AIDS,
like before I kept turning my back to where
the body might want to take me

as if through the cold wind of morning sifting,
warm blood of monthly migraine,
tears of everything we are not,
have not become, have not
made ourselves, all we are not,
cannot come to, cannot sort out, some body
like some god knows what could say
strength, fuck it, and love
let it, take me, it could say, here, have it,
like some body I have always been
waiting for not seeing
it is here.

That day, and most bitter

dies magna et amara

"I know you are reading this poem listening for something, torn
                        between bitterness and hope
turning back once again to the task you cannot refuse.
I know you are reading this poem because there is nothing else
                        left to read
there where you have landed, stripped as you are"
                        (Adrienne Rich – "An Atlas of the Difficult World")

I have taken out the road map, literally, to see
where it might lead
tell me where I should go
way out
to whatever wilderness we can pitch our tent in, where we can
walk;

I've looked at the map
and I've come back to this: this atlas of a difficult world
I can't find my way
toward anything else –

turn back to the task I cannot refuse:
I could call this a poem
but it's simpler and denser
and the only task a poem ever points to
being
life itself.

This is where it carries me, this Atlas,
this other direction from the tight case of

affect, feeling
packed for frugality, scarcity,
this is the thick network of lines,
as in wound and wound about
with who knows where we are heading
though all the riches of the world lie about us,
like disaffection –

call it: the task in hand:
look to my own everyday with those I most need,
back to my own need:

last night I dreamt how sore my hands were
with having built that rampart
those face bricks!
tear it down or let it fall like the wall
at Saumur, chateau we went to,
the two of you – my mother and father –
and I – still almost young –
and what to do with your estrangement
your bickering your bitterness –

forty four years and does it stand still
this ancient stepped wall

I turn to her, this woman of words, this poet's
quiet conviction:
there is nothing left.

Out on the road I have found on the map,
out to the reserve,
time, place, made, assured for the four of us,
find ourselves, one by one, all four of us,
father and mother, son and daughter,

telling our dreams in the morning,
through the grey clearing,
(jackals outside all night clearly calling);
dreams bright and gleaming
as the sword our son must forge for himself
(his father's too heavy, too blunt),
talismans from that place the strange one comes from,
gift to my husband:
"get to know me" –

the whole story,
yours and mine,
and how we end up here,
and how we are here, me, you,
hoping that this isn't an end
bitter with the aftertaste of reconnaissance, revue;

back to the task at hand, take up the map of least
resistance –
what she asks,
this poet: what behoves us;
what reminds me of Anna Akhmatova
recording her requiem,
the long line of mothers
of prisoners, faces I see
torn, stripped, as the Käthe Kollwitz etchings
your father bought you, Mother,
Akhmatova recording her hell,
and your mother
knitting socks for Russia!
o god Mother what behoves us;
(someone stole your mama-bundle
your mother in mother in mother
precious patterned

wooden doll
stolen from the exhibition you'd lent it to;
dutiful daughter, what behoves us?)

the whole story: the story of the ancestors –
am I too weak for it,
too absent minded too absent –
you set me a test I can do nothing
but fail –

your mother, implacable against Afrikaner state hate
determined communist, atheist,
under the auspices of the Anglicans
set up the first secondary school in Marabastad –

it doesn't help,
remonstrance;
I don't know where to turn,
I am so tired, Mother,

remind me:
what fields to walk, what earth, what for –

bitterly
you went down and so bloody
sad

the truth of it so far
beyond me

I dream of it like a stone in the chest
like a woman bent
with death itself:

last night I said to Toekie (your adored,
like a daughter, and dead at thirty)
"it only gets worse"
meaning what?
meaning what
          I can't answer

last night I dreamt death so strongly
I woke in that child-like panic
I woke in before you died –
not quite the dead weight of dread
the day before you did it
but the sweat on Christmas Eve, nine months before,
night of annunciation –
my own death
my own everlasting, always –

you went off to meet death
with one shot, like the lightning
I was so afraid of,
and you, wild and embracing dancing
(as my brother reminds me)
with me (when I was three)
as it crashed about the empty shed;

all run out, all thinned out,
like the body in age,
like justice that can't stand
for truth;
"you'll do the right thing"
you'd say to me –
pity it – bitterest justice –

not only "it isn't fair"
nor your father's law
nor your own, the teaching you did years ago –
fierce internationalist, pacifist –

put it down
this dead weight

the task at hand
what is left

what behoves us
what life asks of us.

Pie Jesu

clear as soprano sung to the treble of a young boy
keeps coming back to me
                                        coming back along
the edge of the water

            the song you loved, listened to, sang to, *Pie Jesu,*

Mother, I could almost laugh now:
all your disavowal

clear as grace notes, silences, *Pie Jesu*

Remember Europe: all the rococo you tracked for us
            country churches, (country cousins, like us –
            our cautious trek across clean, agrarian, Bavaria)
            and inside – this excess, abandon
            of cherubs and gilt, trimmings
            of gold leaf and frillings
            and Mary mother of God lifting completely to
                                                    ecstacy!
            Remember her son's death in Munich –
            Botticelli's weepy, blessed Jesus, and weep I did
            in the open, in front of the painting:
            my own lost love
            and how would it ever rise again –

Mother; for God's sake! how could you ever have told us
            how you didn't believe –
            the words we fumble for to call,
falling back again on the old words you turned your back
against,
all you told us with one voice
wasn't there, all you claimed with reason

you couldn't come to,
                    Christ!
                    nothing! nothing
                    to be gained from this, you let it
all away
                    for nothing.
                    Pie Jesu.

Everlasting light
lux perpetua

Sit in the sun
           and believe

even a day of such still
                  could not hold her back –

body, bend where the burning is
that carries the end of all loveliness,   such a world
as if the sun would never die
                  bend where the hurt is,
                           bend, breathe   body, breathe –

sit in the sun and admit
                  need
                  admit
                  need.
                  Bend body.

how to resurrect you

"don't let them break your spirit"
your words, Mother,
when I was twelve and standing too often
outside the class-room
I am standing outside again
I have been standing for nearly two years
outside of everything
don't break,
spirit, whisper, listen, breathe
bend, how to bring you back
everything you turned your back on

could not bring yourself to believe

what I need
to believe
new life, life again, body love
bring me back,
resurrect me.
Come back.

afterword

Sanctus

Last night my mother came to me;
she had hanged herself
like under the moon of a myth –

the rope, the yoke of necessity –

who took me across the abyss
who called so far so deep
who helped me to those steps

I took them like temple steps –
priestesses, sisters,
assisting, above me –

there she was as she was
in her last days   only she wanted to speak
at last as if at last
she needed to speak
and I turned to the nurses, the sisters
of mercy asking for mercy, let her speak!

Something like death clogging her mouth like a cloth
like that sentence   her last sentence
I didn't hear   didn't stay

head on my arm
my arm supporting her neck
where the head felt the pain
right through the dream –

as if she were dying
as if she were sick

and I, at last
meeting her need –

she lay on my arm and she spoke

her skin thinned
across her cheek
spare, stark
as an Inca queen
in the ice of death –
her teeth flashed gold:

we have done
what we came to do –
it is time –

quiet, at a distance,
my arm supported her head,
as to a child, I whispered
we loved you, you know that,
you loved us, we know this,
as if she were my child, my adored,
my darling, my darling –
she breathed
slow, deep, at last, far, at last
it was only my breathing the whispered
breath only mine as I woke
holding that breathing, nothing stirred –

this was the visit –
she came to me to say
this is it –

her beads said it –

her necklace of Venetian glass,
colours like flowers, trees, a lake
bright against black,

her words said it –
it was time

love, listening, speaking
for all of us, for her clan,
for the first time since she left us,

her breathing said it –
she heard it –
her breathing head
against my arm, her breathing
with the last breath leaving,
hearing love lasting,
her breathing,   mine.